Hobbies/Comic

£2.50

D1099534

mac 2005

Cartoons from the *Daily Mail*

Stan McMurtry **mac**
Edited by Mark Bryant

ROBSON BOOKS

**For my very good friends, Bernard and Franky Cookson,
and also the man with the cakes, Kenneth Mahood**

First published in Great Britain in 2005 by Robson Books,
The Chrysalis Building, Bramley Road, London W10 6SP

An imprint of **Chrysalis** Books Group plc

Copyright © 2005 Stan McMurtry

Selection and text copyright © 2005 Mark Bryant

The right of Stan McMurtry to be identified as the author of this work has been asserted
by him in accordance with the Copyright, Designs and Patents Act 1988

British Library Cataloguing in Publication Data
A catalogue record for this title is available from the British Library

ISBN 1 86105 881 0

All rights reserved. No part of this publication may be reproduced, stored in a retrieval system,
or transmitted in any form or by any means, electronic, mechanical, photocopying, recording or
otherwise, without the prior permission in writing of the publishers.

Typeset by SX Composing DTP, Rayleigh, Essex
Printed and bound in Italy by 🚂 Grafica Veneta S.p.A.

Sir Mark Thatcher, the 51-year-old son of former Conservative Prime Minister Margaret Thatcher, faced 15 years in jail after being charged with helping to finance an attempt to topple the government of oil-rich Equatorial Guinea.

'If you were a real man you'd be out organising a *coup d'état* in some oil-rich African state!'   *27 August 2004*

The 28th Olympiad in Athens closed with a spectacular fireworks display. Britain took 30 medals – 9 gold, 9 silver and 12 bronze – its best Olympics results for 80 years.

'Hey, Dimitri, what're you doing tomorrow? The Prime Minister wants all the stadiums taken down.' *31 August*

Adam Crozier, Chief Executive of Royal Mail, made a public apology after a survey revealed that only six out of 121 post-code areas met delivery targets for first-class mail and that every year 14 million items were lost.

'What rubbish is this? I haven't received any letters of complaint.'   *1 September*

The wayward 18-year-old England football star Wayne Rooney – whose reputation had been sullied by reports of his visits to brothels – joined Alex Ferguson's Manchester United for £27 million, making him the world's most expensive teenage footballer.

'I've just had another look at my contract, boss. What's a eunuch?' *2 September*

Threatened by exposure in an unauthorised biography of the writer and barrister Sir John Mortimer, the actress Wendy Craig revealed to the creator of *Rumpole of the Bailey* that he was the father of her 1960s love-child, now a 42-year-old TV executive.

'Remember way back in 1963, Mr Mortimer? When I was polishin' your study floor wearin' me mini-skirt?'
14 September

As the heated debate on hunting with hounds continued in Parliament, a protester from the paternal rights group Fathers 4 Justice managed to breach royal security and climb onto a ledge at Buckingham Palace, dressed as Batman.

'Ah, Inspector. You're probably wondering why I've called you in here...'   *15 September*

Further security questions were raised when five pro-hunting demonstrators – including the son of rock star Bryan Ferry – stormed the House of Commons.

'Good Lord, no. I'm not an MP – I've been living here for years.' *17 September*

More than 200 walkers gathered at Derbyshire Bridge in the Peak District to celebrate the success of their 'Right to Roam' campaign.

'Darling, these gentlemen are from the Hackney Wick Ramblers' Club and they're exercising their right to roam.' *21 September*

Speaking at a Confederation of British Industry conference, Trade Secretary Patricia Hewitt said it was the national duty of women to have children. Meanwhile, the 72-year-old veteran TV presenter and singer Des O'Connor became a father for the fifth time.

'At your service, ladies. Like Des O'Connor we're keen to do our patriotic duty...'   *23 September*

Britain's biggest insurance company, Norwich Union, announced that it would be moving its call centres to Asia. Meanwhile, research on professional mediums at the University of Hertfordshire failed to prove their ability to communicate with the dead.

'...Sorry...for...the...delay...our...call...centre...has...moved...to...India...' *24 September*

Interviewed about her new portfolio of photos – including one showing her wearing a black dress and 6-inch heels – 44-year-old 'domestic goddess' Nigella Lawson said her advertising tycoon husband Charles Saatchi thought her sexier than Marilyn Monroe.

'You don't have to convince me, darling. So you can stop tottering around on those ridiculous high heels.' *5 October*

There was a public outcry when it was revealed that only 4% of the £750 million of National Lottery money pledged by the Government four years ago to improve school sports facilities had been spent.

'Don't be selfish, Wayne. Other people are waiting to use the new sports facilities.'   *6 October*

The 2004 edition of the *Eurostat Yearbook* – the EU's 'statistical compendium' – was published with a picture of Great Britain on its cover, minus Wales.

'So that EU map was right!'   *7 October*

As his pregnant wife announced that their third child was expected in March, further news broke of David Beckham's infidelities when the 22-year-old owner of an Essex beauty salon claimed to have had an affair with the England football captain.

'Y'know, Marge, if things don't get any better I may have to have sex with David Beckham and sell my story.' *12 October*

A 60-year-old grandmother rescued a man who was being attacked by a 14-foot crocodile in Queensland, Australia. Meanwhile, in Britain, animal rights protesters dug up the body of a woman whose family bred guinea pigs for medical research.

'Don't rescue any more people tonight, Alice. We've got that loony British animal rights group on the phone.' *13 October*

A report by Adair Turner, head of the Government's Pensions Commission, said that to plug the £57-billion black hole in public and private pensions provision, men and women would have to delay their retirement ages to 70 and 67, respectively.

'Damn! He's got away!' *14 October*

A probationary member of the exclusive Wentworth Golf Club in Surrey had her application turned down when it was revealed that she had once worked as a topless model.

'All agreed? Another five minutes and if the committee hasn't reinstated that ex-topless model we'll go in for a nice hot cup of tea.' *15 October*

Health Secretary John Reid was accused of a cover-up when a confidential report on passive smoking by the Government's Scientific Committee on Tobacco and Health was leaked. It said that passive smoking was a 'substantial public health hazard'.

'It won't affect me. I always order my husband outside to smoke.'   *19 October*

There was widespread criticism of the anti-social consequences of the Gambling Bill, which could put a Las Vegas-style 'super casino' filled with big-money slot machines in every British town and earn the Treasury £260 million a year in tax revenue.

'More housekeeping money? Dammit, Sarah, I've only just forked out for a new kitchen.' *21 October*

Twenty-year-old Prince Harry hit the headlines when he lashed out at a photographer after leaving a London nightclub in the early hours of the morning.

'I fear you may have a long wait, Sleeping Beauty. The handsome prince is engaged upon royal duties – getting plastered in nightclubs and beating up photographers.' *22 October*

At a meeting of EU interior ministers in Luxembourg, Home Secretary David Blunkett agreed to sign away Britain's power to veto new European laws on immigration and asylum but insisted that this would not affect UK border controls.

'Of course we'll still retain control of our bord—'   *26 October*

At a ceremony in Balaclava, Ukraine, to mark the 150th anniversary of the Charge of the Light Brigade, the 83-year-old Duke of Edinburgh wore sunglasses to cover up a black eye he claimed was the result of a fall in his hotel bathroom.

'I'll tell everyone he slipped in the bath. But I'm warning you, Harry – don't you dare take your grandfather nightclubbing again!'   *27 October*

As it was revealed that planning applications had been received for 125 'super casinos', a village in Buckinghamshire became the latest victim of the travellers' invasion that was blighting Britain's rural communities.

'Damned travellers, polluting our town! Whatever next?' *28 October*

Nature magazine reported that Australian scientists working on an island in Indonesia had discovered the remains of seven tiny humanoid prehistoric creatures. Only 3 feet tall, the bodies dated from *c*.16,000 BC.

'Gosh. A whirlwind romance in Indonesia? When can we meet the lucky man?' *29 October*

Plans unveiled in the Government's Children Bill would mean that parents caught smacking their children severely enough to mark the skin could face up to five years in jail. Meanwhile, the crucial final debate on hunting with hounds approached.

'I think it's instead of smacking.' *3 November*

After two members of the Metropolitan Police were suspended for shooting dead a 46-year-old father of three – mistaking a Queen Anne-style table leg he was carrying for a shotgun – Scotland Yard marksmen threatened to go on strike.

'Great news, sir. The gun strike has been called off.' *4 November*

In the US presidential elections, George W Bush swept back into the White House with an unprecedented wave of support from right-wing fundamentalist Christian groups, notably those in the eleven states that banned gay marriages.

'Shucks, honey. Ah have bad news. We may have to wait another four years.' *5 November*

Environmental campaigners and rural communities were shocked when Deputy Prime Minister John Prescott announced plans to build a further 130,000 new homes across the south-east of England at a time when thousands of properties in the area stood empty.

'Sadly, since John Prescott took all our land for housing,
Bernard's thinking seriously of getting out of farming.' *10 November*

A French pharmaceutical company claimed that its new wonder pill, Accomplia, could help people lose weight, stop smoking and reduce their cravings for alcohol all at the same time.

'My husband gave me a miracle pill guaranteed to make me lose weight and stop smoking and drinking – it was called cyanide.' *11 November*

Married father-of-four Boris Johnson – editor of the *Spectator* and a Conservative MP – was accused of having an affair with a journalist colleague.

'Oh dear. It's another confused and befuddled man who's been acting strangely, dumped by his wife.' *16 November*

The House of Commons supported a total ban on fox-hunting. Meanwhile, Health Secretary John Reid introduced a Government White Paper on Public Health that would ban smoking in all workplaces, restaurants and pubs which serve food.

'Okay, so the good news is they're almost certain to ban hunting – what's the bad news?'   *17 November*

In what many felt was interference by a 'nanny state', John Reid's White Paper also advocated clearer warnings of health risks on product labels and the introduction of helplines to give advice on diet, nutrition, exercise and even sex.

'Wow. What a night! Off to the pub for a Diet Coke and a longing look at the cigarette machine, then back to my place for some muesli and to watch my pet rabbits having sex.' *18 November*

In an unfair dismissal case brought by a former member of Prince Charles's household it was revealed that the Prince had said: 'What is it that makes everyone seem to think they are qualified to do things beyond their technical capabilities?'

'You want to be King? What is it, Charles, that makes everyone think they are qualified to do things far beyond their capabilities?' *19 November*

Home Secretary David Blunkett launched a legal bid to prove that he was the father of his pregnant former lover's baby and her two-year-old son, and declared he was prepared to go to court to demand DNA tests.

'It's great news. I'm not sure if it was that pedigree cocker spaniel or the scruffy mongrel from next door but one.'
23 November

The Government announced plans to introduce compulsory identity cards to help guard against terrorism. Meanwhile, Buckingham Palace's security was tightened after another fathers' rights protester scaled a 20-foot gatepost and chained himself to it.

'Come on, come on. How are we to know you're not Al Qaeda? Where's your ID card?' *24 November*

Tony Blair was accused of fuelling the politics of fear when he announced the introduction of further national-security measures including the formation of a 5,000-strong British version of the FBI to be called the Serious Organised Crime Agency (SOCA).

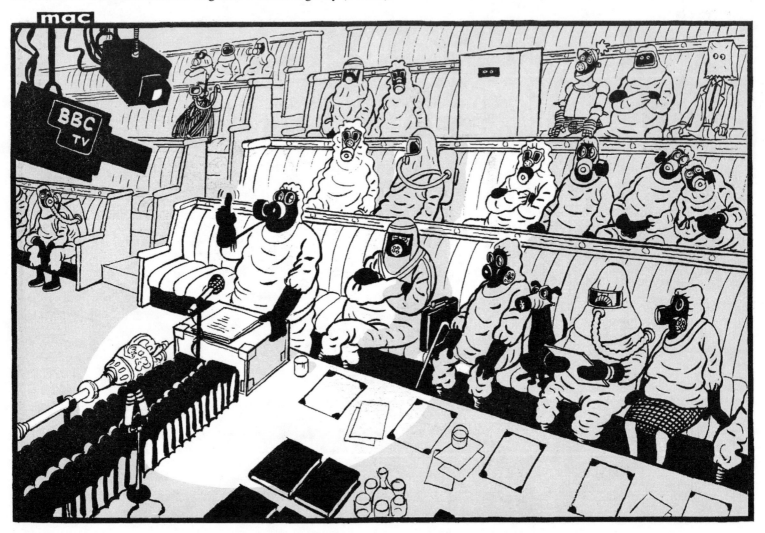

'...Furthermore this Government has been accused of creating a climate of fear...what nonsense. Who would stoop so low?' *25 November*

In addition to the creation of the Serious Organised Crime Agency, the Government granted extended powers to the recently formed civilian Community Support Officers.

'That's right, sir. The blue ones are the new Community Support Officers' speed cameras, and the red ones are run by the Serious Organised Crime Agency – you've just been nicked by a police yellow one.' *26 November*

Sensational home-video tapes of Princess Diana – in which she revealed intimate details of her relationship with Prince Charles – were broadcast in the USA. Meanwhile, in Britain, further details emerged about David Blunkett's sex life.

'How can a stranger understand? You don't know what it's like to have your sex life aired in public.'   *1 December*

Home Secretary David Blunkett announced that he would rather give up his Cabinet post than his fight for access to the children he believed were his.

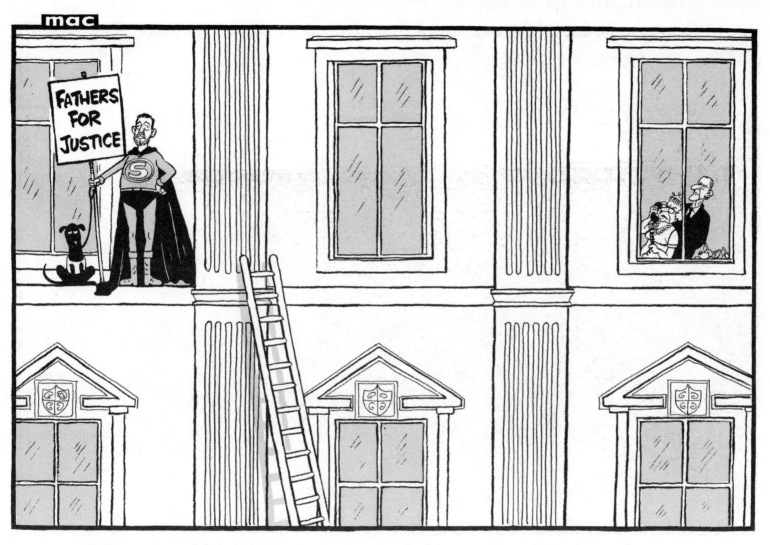

'Mr Blair, will you kindly come and remove your Home Secretary from my window ledge?'   *2 December*

After police chiefs called for greater rights for individuals to protect their homes from intruders, a new Householders Protection Bill was introduced under which people would only be prosecuted if the 'degree of force was grossly disproportionate'.

'George, I have an uneasy feeling those burglars sneaking up our path who you've just used reasonable force on were carol singers.' *7 December*

In an attempt to get the debt-laden BBC back into the black, Director General Mark Thompson announced cuts of £320 million and a 15% reduction in the corporation's 28,000 workforce.

'...That was the news...and now, instead of the football, some more cooking tips from Mr Wonky Bear...' *8 December*

In what was seen as a 'living will', Hammersmith Hospital Trust in London introduced a controversial 'tick the box and die' scheme for elderly patients, by which they were able to request that they should be allowed to die if they became terminally ill.

'Attention, everybody. Before cook serves up her pre-Christmas lunch does anyone want to tick the "I want to die" box?' *14 December*

As the 'living will' Bill was discussed by Parliament, a Government-commissioned report into the pensions crisis said that if employees failed to save for their pensions, the current system would soon have to be scrapped.

'...So as you haven't saved for a pension, Cyril, we've all clubbed together and bought you some cyanide pills.' *15 December*

The annual school league tables report showed an increase in truancy, with one in five pupils skipping classes. Meanwhile, the Prime Minister pledged £519 million to give every child access to at least four hours of sport each week.

'Sir, I think the headmistress would like a word.' *16 December*

After claims that he had fast-tracked a visa for his lover's nanny, Home Secretary David Blunkett resigned. He was replaced by former Education Secretary Charles Clarke.

'I wouldn't sit there yet. Mr Blunkett's dog was very upset about leaving.' *17 December*

In the biggest bank robbery in criminal history, £27 million in cash was stolen from the headquarters of the Northern Bank in Belfast. Meanwhile, it was revealed that 40% of Britain's cash machines now charge users for making withdrawals.

'...And don't you go using them cash machines either. They're daylight bloody robbery!'   *23 December*

A damning study by researchers at Newcastle University attacked official crime statistics and claimed that Britain's police forces are 'the worst in the developed world', adding that people are 30 times more likely to be robbed today than they were in the 1960s.

'What a start to 2005. Named as the worst police force in the world...How was your day, darling?' *4 January 2005*

In a widely condemned move, the National Parks Authority announced plans to axe guided walks in the Lake District because they attracted too many 'middle-aged, middle-class white people' and not enough urban youth, ethnic minorities and disabled people.

'In two words, Sajeed. How would we like to help make nine-mile treks around the Lake District less white and middle class?' *5 January*

The hook-handed radical Muslim preacher Abu Hamza, accused of incitement to racial hatred, failed to appear in court at London's Old Bailey because he said he was unable to walk as his toenails had grown too long.

'The chiropodist is here, Mr Hamza.' *6 January*

Older women claimed they were being discriminated against in favour of more-glamorous younger players when it emerged that seven of the eight players invited to take part in the World Bowls Tour Women's Matchplay event were aged between 21 and 37.

'Even if they do get you into the team, Cynthia, what are you going to bowl with?'   *7 January*

As Gordon Brown embarked on a trip to Africa to highlight Britain's role in combating Third World poverty, a new book – *Brown's Britain* by Robert Peston – revealed details of the long-standing feud between the Chancellor and Prime Minister Tony Blair.

'Psst, look – din-dins!' *11 January*

Despite condemnation from police chiefs and doctors who feared an increase in drunken violence among Britain's youth, Culture Secretary Tessa Jowell announced that the new Licensing Act which allowed 24-hour drinking would take effect in February.

'All this fuss. I've been 24-hour drinking for years and it hasn't done me any harm, has it, lads?' *13 January*

Prince Harry was forced to make a public apology after appearing at a friend's fancy-dress party dressed as a Nazi soldier at a time when Jewish groups were marking the 60th anniversary of the liberation of Auschwitz concentration camp.

'For future reference, Baddely, the correct form of address is "Good morning, Your Royal Highness", not "Heil Harry".' *14 January*

After nine years of fertility treatment, a 66-year-old retired university professor from Romania gave birth to a 3-pound girl, making her the world's oldest mother.

'Oh dear. I'd like to chat a bit longer but I think the baby is on its way.' *18 January*

As the nation prepared itself for 24-hour drinking, the Government was accused of a cover-up when a leaked official report into Accident & Emergency units in Britain's hospitals revealed that 7 out of 10 patients admitted after midnight were drunk.

'Sorry, sir. We're fully booked at 2am tomorrow. If you could delay getting paralytic and injured until about 3.15, we have a vacancy then.' *19 January*

Shocking photographs were published showing the abuse of Iraqi prisoners by British soldiers at Camp Breadbasket, near Basra, after the end of the Iraq war.

Army Recruitment *20 January*

The four-year-old, 76,000-ton P&O superliner *Aurora* – carrying 1,374 passengers who had paid up to £42,000 each for a 93-day world cruise – broke down after sailing only 110 miles from Southampton.

'Oops. Silly me. I've been leaving the choke knob out.' *21 January*

Prince Andrew faced a ban on using taxpayers' money for private trips when an official report from the National Audit Office revealed that 'Air Miles Andy' had spent £325,000 in a single year on hiring aircraft to fly to golf matches and other events.

'Could you move your buggy back a bit, Prince Andrew? It's on my ball.' *25 January*

Police were criticised for spending £10,000 in a court battle involving a woman who had been arrested for holding an apple while driving. Meanwhile, four Britons who had been held at the US prison camp in Guantanamo Bay, Cuba, arrived back in the UK.

'Come on, come on! Have you at any time driven a car while holding an apple in your hand?'   *26 January*

A Home Office survey revealed that three-quarters of Britain's criminals were never caught, only one in 100 ever went to trial, violent crime had increased by 6% and gun crime was up by 5%.

'I'm just popping down to the bank. Is there anything you want from the shops?' *27 January*

The 44-year-old radical Muslim cleric Abu Qatada – who claimed £1,000 a month in benefits – was released from Belmarsh high-security prison, where he had been held under new emergency terror laws. He was then tagged and placed under house arrest.

'At first you might find they chafe your ankles a bit when you go out to get your benefits, Mr Qatada.' *28 January*

Following a series of high-profile cases, the Government issued a new booklet, 'Householders and the Use of Force Against Intruders', to clarify householders' rights to defend themselves and their property against burglars.

'Be gentle, Bernard. "Section A. Clause B. Do not continue the assault after you have rendered the burglar unconscious..."' *2 February*

Less than a month after quitting the UK Independence Party, the 62-year-old former TV presenter Robert Kilroy-Silk launched his new political party, Veritas, with an attack on multiculturalism in Britain.

'Hang on, dear. That wasn't a burglar. It was somebody called Kilroy-Silk canvassing for a new party.' *3 February*

A new slimming drink was launched, which its manufacturer claimed could also boost people's love lives. Meanwhile, the Orgasmatron, an electrical device designed to improve women's sexual satisfaction, began clinical trials in the USA.

'Now concentrate, Vera. Which turns you on most, the slimming drink or the Orgasmatron?' *4 February*

The 28-year-old Briton Ellen MacArthur returned home after breaking the record for sailing solo, non-stop, around the world. Her 71-day, 27,000-mile trip in a 75-foot-long trimaran broke the previous record by more than a day.

'It's Ellen MacArthur. She can't adjust to sleeping at home.' *9 February*

More than 30 years after their romance began, Prince Charles and his mistress, Camilla Parker Bowles, announced that they would be married in April.

'Go for it, Sharon. This means there's going to be a vacancy for a mistress.' *11 February*

After much discussion it was agreed that Prince Charles's new wife would be addressed as 'HRH the Duchess of Cornwall', but it was still unclear whether she would become Queen if and when Prince Charles accedes to the throne.

'It's your mother, sir. Did Mrs Parker Bowles accidentally pick up the wrong hat when you last visited?' *15 February*

In a high-profile divorce case, the former wife of dotcom millionaire Jonathan Rowland also claimed a share of the £690-million fortune of her former father-in-law, City financier David Rowland, one of the richest men in Britain.

'Now, William. Say after me… "With all my worldly goods I thee endow, including half my father's house, stocks, shares and bank accounts".' *16 February*

The last legal day of fox-hunting with hounds in Britain was marked by a defiant call to action by thousands of hunters who vowed to defy the ban.

'What're you in for, mate?' *18 February*

There was a toxic-food alert and nearly 400 products were withdrawn from supermarkets when the illegal dye Sudan 1 was discovered in a batch of chilli powder used to make Worcestershire Sauce, a basic ingredient of many own-brand ready-meals.

'Attention. You are handling a highly toxic food product. Replace on shelf, remove clothing and step into the decontamination unit in aisle three.' *22 February*

The Prevention of Terrorism Bill was published, allowing police to place suspects under house arrest without trial. Meanwhile, icy weather suddenly gripped the country after what had been Britain's mildest winter for 15 years.

'Aw. Shame we can't leave the house. Another dreary evening ahead sitting by the fire toasting crumpets and drinking tea...'

23 February

Buckingham Palace reported that the Queen would not attend Prince Charles's civil wedding to Camilla Parker Bowles at the Guildhall, Windsor, but added that she would be present at a blessing service in Windsor Castle after the ceremony

'Picture their faces, ma'am, if at the last moment you burst out of the cake shouting, "Surprise, surprise!"'   *24 February*

Following an Appeal Court ruling on human rights, a 16-year-old Muslim girl from Luton, Bedfordshire, won the right to wear head-to-toe Islamic dress at school.

'You'd probably get away with it, Samantha, if you weren't a white Catholic from Croydon.' *3 March*

When Prince Charles landed in Alice Springs as part of his Australian tour, he was greeted with a welcome dance by six elderly women from the Papunya tribe, five of whom were topless, painted with red ochre and wore turkey feathers in their hair.

'Honestly, Camilla. I had no idea. What I thought was a dance of welcome turned out to be a marriage ceremony.' *4 March*

A victim of its own popularity, it emerged that there was a funding crisis at London's world-renowned Great Ormond Street Hospital for Children, which meant that it would have to close a fifth of its beds, cancel operations and cut staff.

'Thanks. But I'm afraid there's still not quite enough.' *8 March*

Researchers at the University of Maryland in Baltimore, USA, claimed that laughter can be good for your health because it makes blood vessels expand and thus helps blood flow, which as a result reduces the risk of heart attacks and strokes.

'I'm sorry your operation has been cancelled again. But have you heard the one about the Englishman, the Irishman and the donkey with one leg?' *9 March*

There was an angry backlash from rural communities when Deputy Prime Minister John Prescott appeared to go easy on gypsies and travellers who set up campsites in the countryside without gaining official planning permission.

'John Prescott's garden? Of course, sir. Turn right, over the bridge, first left then straight through the gate.' *10 March*

The Lord Chancellor, Lord Falconer, announced plans for a new 'marriage lite' law, which would give unmarried live-in couples the same legal rights to property and financial maintenance following a split as those enjoyed by married couples.

'Thanks for a wonderful evening, Jeremy. It's been lovely to meet you. My lawyers will be in touch.' *15 March*

Chancellor Gordon Brown's 'giveaway' Budget – the last before the General Election –
contained many sweeteners for businesses and the general public. However, City experts
warned that taxes would have to rise after the election.

'Oops! I'm terribly sorry, I appear to have brought my "after the election" Budget speech by mistake.' *16 March*

In an attempt to stem rising school drop-out rates and improve literacy, Gordon Brown also unveiled new Education Maintenance Allowances of £75 a week to encourage youngsters to stay in full-time education or training.

'I bet it says fags are up again.' *17 March*

Jamie Oliver's TV show *Jamie's School Dinners* highlighted the horrors of junk-food school meals, and a 125,000-signature petition the chef presented to 10 Downing Street led to a reappraisal of the nutritional quality of food served to schoolchildren.

'My compliments to Mr Blair on the temporary improvements. But the Châteauneuf du Pape is corked.' *22 March*

After considerable debate, Constitutional Affairs Minister Christopher Leslie confirmed that Camilla Parker Bowles would become Queen if and when Prince Charles accedes to the throne.

'Are you absolutely sure she'd get custody of the corgis?' *23 March*

A man from Sydenham, south London, was attacked in his back garden by a 'black panther' the size of a Labrador dog when he went to rescue his pet cat in the early hours of the morning.

'Hang on, I'll get him. He's feeding the cat.'   *24 March*

To combat the country's two million uninsured and untaxed 'rogue drivers', police introduced new number-plate recognition technology and planned a huge increase in roadside cameras, making Britain one of the most spied-on societies on Earth.

'Don't worry. Your husband won't be back for hours. I've got him setting up new hi-tech cameras on every street corner.' *25 March*

In order for Prince Charles to receive the official blessing of the Church on his wedding, the Bishop of Salisbury called for him to publicly apologise to Camilla Parker Bowles's first husband for committing adultery with his wife.

'Ah, Simpkins. Pop out and lob this house brick through Mr Parker Bowles's window, will you?'   *29 March*

As the 2005 General Election debate gathered momentum, Tory Party leader Michael Howard attacked Labour's 'total failure' to deal with immigration and pledged to set up a Border Control Police Force accountable to a new Minister of Homeland Security.

30 March

During a holiday photocall with his sons at the Swiss ski resort of Klosters, Prince Charles was unwittingly recorded muttering his loathing of the media, calling them 'bloody people'.

'I don't think any more "bloody people" will be bothering them for a while.'   *1 April*

After hearing evidence against six Birmingham councillors who rigged postal votes in the 2004 local elections, a High Court judge condemned the Government's failure to implement new measures to tackle similar fraud ahead of the General Election.

'Okay, if there's nobody in there waiting to alter the postal votes, why the regular chicken and chips?' *6 April*

Shortly after the royal wedding had to be postponed because of the funeral of Pope John Paul II – which would be attended by the Prime Minister and the Archbishop of Canterbury – the death of Prince Rainier III of Monaco was announced.

'Prince Rainier's funeral has been brought forward to this Saturday, sir – and you're invited.'   *7 April*

As election fever mounted, Liberal Democrat leader Charles Kennedy and his wife, Sarah, showed off their first baby, Donald James, who was born at St Thomas' Hospital, London.

'Oh, no! He's been canvassing on behalf of his dad already!'   *13 April*

In a speech to launch the Labour Party's new manifesto, Tony Blair confounded Gordon Brown's supporters by declaring that he intended to serve for a full third term if re-elected. Meanwhile, new research showed that aspirin could stave off heart attacks.

'Yes, folks. I will be serving another full term as Prime Minister.' *14 April*

As Labour pledged to increase the number of new hospitals in Britain, the actress Leslie Ash – who nearly died after contracting a hospital superbug – said on BBC Radio 4's *Today* programme that not enough was being done to stop the MRSA epidemic.

'There are some superbugs at the door canvassing for Labour and their promise of a hundred new hospitals by 2010.'

15 April

As the crisis in Britain's hospitals deepened, Labour leaders claimed that Conservative election plans for the health service would result in patients paying huge sums for treatment and would threaten the very existence of the NHS itself.

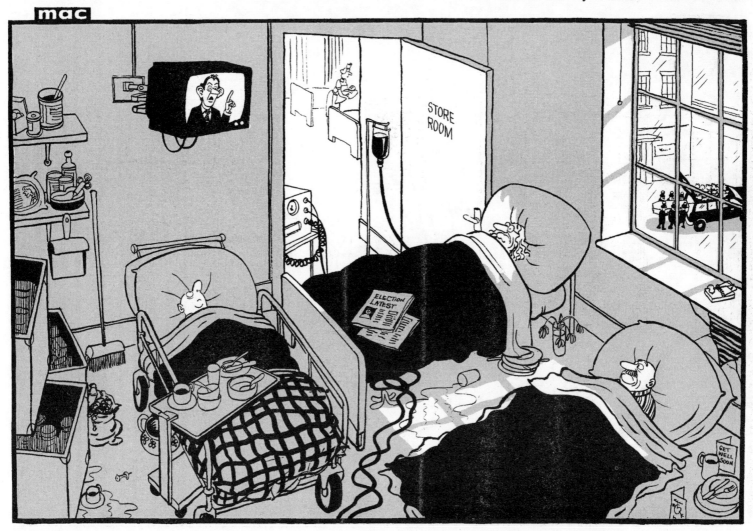

'Remember, folks. Voting for the Conservatives would mean an end to the NHS as we know it.' *19 April*

After only two days' deliberation, 78-year-old Cardinal Joseph Ratzinger of Germany was elected Pope Benedict XVI. The oldest pope for 300 years, he was also the first German to hold the post for a millennium.

'Be nice to the lad, Bernard – he really wanted that job.'   *21 April*

In an experiment to tackle absenteeism, Royal Mail workers who did not take any days off sick over a period of six months were entered into a prize draw. As a result 37 employees received a £12,000 car and 75 others received £2,000 holiday vouchers.

'Sad, isn't it? If he goes sick he has to hand back his shiny new car.' *26 April*

Following a risk-assessment study on Prince Charles's new wife, the Duchess of Cornwall was given a new SAS-trained female police bodyguard.

'Charles, dear, would you tell Camilla that her in-laws have popped in for a cup of tea and to mention this to her new bodyguard?'   *27 April*

After the leaking of the Attorney General's report on the legality of the invasion of Iraq, Tony Blair and Labour leaders were accused of lying to the British people over the reasons for going to war, a claim they strenuously denied.

'Good morning, young lady. I'm so pleased to meet you in your beautiful home and hey! What a lovely little doggy...'   *28 April*

The world's biggest passenger jet – the 239-foot-long Airbus A380 – made its maiden flight in
Toulouse, France. Built in Britain, France, Germany and Spain, the luxury plane can seat
850 passengers and has bars, showers, casinos and even a gym.

'Time to fasten your seatbelt, sir. The front end has landed.' *29 April*

Researchers from Oxford University's Department of Physiology reported that junk-food diets are linked to aggressive behaviour and learning difficulties in children. Meanwhile, political campaigning intensified as the General Election approached.

'Answer the door, son – but don't bite anybody from Labour. It makes you aggressive.'   *3 May*

New statistics revealed that senior managers were the fastest-growing section of NHS staff – up by more than two-thirds to 36,000 in 2004. Over the same period the number of nurses rose by 23% and doctors by 29%.

'All right. Anybody else who hasn't postal-voted for Labour?' *4 May*

On his first day as an officer cadet at the Royal Military Academy, Sandhurst, Prince Harry declared that he wanted to be treated like any other new recruit.

'Twenty miles to go, squad. But first, certain little home comforts are going to have to be dispensed with…'   *10 May*

A leaked internal audit by Lloyds TSB bank, and a subsequent TV documentary, revealed that in order to meet personal sales targets and boost their own salaries, staff at many British banks gave loans to people who could not afford them.

'You heard me, buster. Take out a loan!'   *11 May*

'Pop the kettle on, darling. Look who was downstairs. It's that nice young man I keep meeting in court...' *12 May*

British MP George Galloway threatened legal action over claims by US senators that he had accepted gifts from Saddam Hussein. Meanwhile, in California, the trial of pop star Michael Jackson began with allegations that he had shared a bed with children.

'Come on, come on! Did you ever share Michael Jackson's bed or give presents to wee George Galloway?' *13 May*

After a number of high-profile reports of brutal attacks and yobbish drunken behaviour in the Greater Manchester area, the city's Chief Superintendent said that gangs of 'feral' hooded youths were terrorising communities in the north of England.

'Hush, dear. Daddy loves these programmes about wildlife in Britain.' *19 May*

A 38-year-old woman from Derby was condemned for running a 'baby factory' that enabled her to receive more than £31,000 a year in state benefits. All three of her teenage daughters had children, the youngest giving birth at the age of 12.

25 May

French President Jacques Chirac's plans for a European superstate were in ruins when a referendum in France rejected the proposed new EU constitution.

'Okay. Now someone who hasn't been eating garlic try giving him the kiss of life.' *31 May*

After the Live 8 international music spectacular to highlight world poverty, Sir Bob Geldof asked sailors to ferry protesters across the Channel in small boats so they could demonstrate at the G8 summit of leaders of the world's richest nations, taking place in Edinburgh.

'*Bonjour*, darling. Bob Geldof invites *vous* to join *mon ami* and *moi sur le voyage* over *le* Channel to throw ze rotten eggs in Edinburgh.' *8 June*

In a drive to clean up Britain's streets, the Government gave local councils tough new powers, including on-the-spot fines of £50 for dropping litter, cigarette butts and chewing gum.

'Psst! I dropped a toffee-wrapper. Can you lend me £50 till tomorrow?' *9 June*

A 56-year-old woman from Gloucestershire, who enjoyed performing her housework naked, objected to the building of new flats overlooking her home on the grounds that her new neighbours would be able to see her in the nude.

'I don't care how you do your housework at home, Mrs Winkley. Here at United Conglomerates we keep our kit on!'   *10 June*

To help working families, Education Secretary Ruth Kelly introduced a new scheme known as 'Kelly Hours' that would keep primary schools open from 8am to 6pm, offering supervised breakfasts and after-school activities such as sport and art.

'Oi! Can't you read?' *14 June*

After a trial lasting four months, singer Michael Jackson was cleared of all charges against him involving child molestation at his Neverland ranch in California.

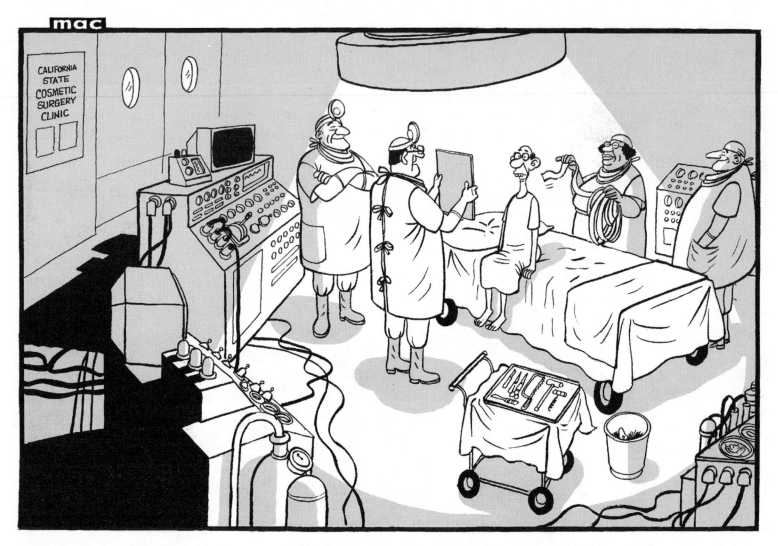

'That's what you said, Michael: "I wanna sell Neverland and become completely anonymous till things blow over."' *15 June*

Royal Ascot was moved to York to allow the racecourse to be redeveloped.

'Oh, you don't understand one's accent? Try this: By 'eck, lad. T'bugger coom in fust. Fifty smackers or ah'll set t'corgi on tha!' *16 June*

After 22 years as a Wimbledon referee, Alan Mills retired. In his autobiography, *Lifting the Covers*, he complained about the recent increase in grunting by female players, claiming it was unsporting and was deliberately used to put off opponents.

'New balls, please!' *21 June*

Three paintings created nearly 50 years ago by a chimpanzee called Congo, as part of a televised experiment in animal behaviour on Desmond Morris's *Zoo Time* programme, fetched £14,750 at auction.

'No, no, no! Start again. This is the kind of stuff that sells for £15,000.' *22 June*

The annual Royal Public Finances Report revealed that Prince Charles and Prince Andrew spent £1.5 million of taxpayers' money on travel last year, while the Queen and Prince Philip spent only £392,000.

'Another drain on the public purse! Do you know how much those tandems cost?' *23 June*

To mark the bicentenary of the death of Lord Nelson, an international flotilla of 167 ships re-enacted the French defeat at the Battle of Trafalgar in front of the Queen at Portsmouth. To avoid triumphalism, the opponents were called the Blue Fleet and the Red Fleet.

'I think that must be a French ship.' *29 June*

At a meeting with Germany's Gerhard Schroeder and Russia's Vladimir Putin shortly before the opening of the G8 summit at the Gleneagles Hotel, Edinburgh, French President Jacques Chirac criticised British cooking, unaware that he was being recorded.

'You'd better hide. Chirac's decided there is something he likes to eat over here after all.' *6 July*

On 6 July, London won the bid to host the 2012 Olympics. The area allotted for the main buildings was an urban wasteland in the Stratford district of the East End.

'That's right. Overlooking where the main Olympic Stadium will be. Will you be wanting the deluxe suite or the standard?'

7 July

The day after winning the 2012 Olympics bid, terrorists struck in the capital, killing 52 people and injuring around 700.

First Gold Medal   *8 July*

Developers offered gardeners in Nottingham £28,000 each to give up their allotments on a 25-acre site, but not all were keen on the deal.

'What're you planting?'   *13 July*

In Weston-super-Mare, near Bristol, a 70-year-old grandmother-of-three married a 31-year-old organist.

'Patience, everybody – here comes one now.' *14 July*

Consumer groups attacked Thames Water and other water companies in the south-east that had asked the public to conserve water, when it was revealed that 800 million gallons a day were being lost through leakage.

'Due to extensive modernisation costs they're putting our water rates up.'   *15 July*

The Home Office and Metropolitan Police launched an appeal after a High Court judge ruled that the new 'child curfew zones' – from which under-16s could be removed by police between 9pm and 6am – infringed children's human rights.

'To celebrate your decision, m'lud. Are you free tonight to nick a couple of motors, go down the club, chat up the totty and get legless with the lads?' *21 July*

After details were published of the latest of the many affairs of Shane Warne – the 35-year-old Australian spin-bowler, captain of Hampshire Cricket Club and father of three – his wife filed for divorce.

'And yet again Shane Warne is taking a much longer run-up than usual.' *22 July*

A 47-year-old cowboy plumber was fined £5,000 and sentenced to 150 hours' community service after he was filmed urinating into a vase and washing it in a customer's water tank during a 'sting' operation set up by trading standards officers.

'Okay, Henry. The plumber's here now. You know what to do if he tries to pee in the water tank.' *28 July*